YOUR KNOWLE[

- We will publish your bachelor's and master's thesis, essays and papers

- Your own eBook and book - sold worldwide in all relevant shops

- Earn money with each sale

Upload your text at www.GRIN.com and publish for free

Liwia Kolodziej

Model-directed Learning. Albert Bandura's Social Cognitive Learning Theory and its Social-psychological Significance for School and Instruction

GRIN Publishing

Bibliographic information published by the German National Library:

The German National Library lists this publication in the National Bibliography; detailed bibliographic data are available on the Internet at http://dnb.dnb.de .

This book is copyright material and must not be copied, reproduced, transferred, distributed, leased, licensed or publicly performed or used in any way except as specifically permitted in writing by the publishers, as allowed under the terms and conditions under which it was purchased or as strictly permitted by applicable copyright law. Any unauthorized distribution or use of this text may be a direct infringement of the author s and publisher s rights and those responsible may be liable in law accordingly.

Imprint:

Copyright © 2006 GRIN Verlag GmbH
Print and binding: Books on Demand GmbH, Norderstedt Germany
ISBN: 978-3-656-88129-2

This book at GRIN:

http://www.grin.com/en/e-book/288024/model-directed-learning-albert-banduras-social-cognitive-learning-theory

GRIN - Your knowledge has value

Since its foundation in 1998, GRIN has specialized in publishing academic texts by students, college teachers and other academics as e-book and printed book. The website www.grin.com is an ideal platform for presenting term papers, final papers, scientific essays, dissertations and specialist books.

Visit us on the internet:

http://www.grin.com/

http://www.facebook.com/grincom

http://www.twitter.com/grin_com

Model-directed Learning

Albert Bandura's Social Cognitive Learning Theory and its Social-psychological Significance for School and Instruction

by Liwia Kolodziej

1. Introduction 3
2. Social cognitive learning theory 4
   2.1. Theoretical framework 4
   2.2. Learning from role models 6
   2.3. Theory of behavior modification 11
3. Social-psychological aspects in school and instruction 14
   3.1. Social relationships in the classroom 14
   3.2. Teacher-student-interaction 15
   3.3. Social learning in school and instruction 18
   3.4. Teacher as model 19
4. Summary: Pedagogical implications of the social cognitive learning theory for school and instruction 21
Literature 23

Cover image: pixabay.com

1. Introduction

This term paper explores the subject „Model-directed Learning, Bandura's social cognitive Learning Theory and its social-psychological Significance for School and Instruction". The topic touches on several complex scientific areas that cannot be exhaustively discussed and in part can only contribute in a more generalized form to the scope of this term paper. Hence, there is the challenge of setting boundaries at first. The main focus of this paper is on the social cognitive learning theory according to Albert Bandura, with its central statements serving as the theoretical foundation of the paper as a whole. The aim is to investigate, which basic principles Bandura is adopting from human behavior, how he does explain and analyze this approach. This theoretical rationale should be set up in the socio-psychological context of school and instruction. Hence, a main goal of this paper is to establish a theory-practice relevance. In other words, the focus is to investigate which consequences are arising from the social cognitive learning theory for school, teaching, education, and studying.

A key aspect of the social cognitive learning theory is model-based learning, thus, the assumption that human learning can happen through observation and imitation of others. In a society, in which humans strive for individuality and originality, imitation and simulation are associated with negative characteristics. Nevertheless, imitation behavior plays an important role even in every day situations. A person's aggressive behavior or drug habit is often rationalized with the assumption that this behavior was copied from friends, or was due to the influence of others, or being surrounded with the wrong people. This term paper attempts to show the scientific reasoning behind this "everyday wisdom", to in part rebut and analyze it. Social-psychological aspects in school and instruction will be used to characterize the relationship between social interactions at school, social learning at school, and learning through imitation, including the role of teacher behavior in this context.

Researching this topic will serve as a reflection for my goal to become a teacher.

I would like to emphasize that this work does solely focus on central general scientific data. Of course, many of these results can be refined in a way that is specific to a situation.

2. Social cognitive learning theory

In general, the social cognitive learning theory by Albert Bandura focusses on questions as to how human beings learn behavioral patterns and how they interact among themselves and with their environment. Hereby not only the reaction of the individual to his environment plays a pivotal role, but also the thought processes, i.e. cognitive operations resulting from human interaction with the environment.

Consequently, Bandura's social cognitive learning theory attempts to integrate behaviorist and cognitivist educational theories, allowing to explain, to analyze and to understand complex social learning. Per definiton social learning is learning of certain behavioral patterns that are causing social recognition or social disdain. Which interaction processes between individual and environment during this learning of behavioral patterns take center stage is the subject of social cognitive learning theory. This chapter focusses on the theoretical principles of the social cognitive learning theory, as described by Bandura in his 1979 publication of the same title.

2.1. Theoretical framework

In order to be able to comprehend Bandura's theories of social cognitive learning and to understand its significance for the complex field of research encompassing education, a classification of learning theory contexts is necessary at first. Learning theorists of the brand of radical behaviorism focus their research mainly on the environmental impacts that human behavior is subjected to (though in their experiments the test subjects were predominantly animals, for example see Skinner). Consequently, the perception was created that an individual was randomly at the mercy of the environment, defined by it and could be arbitrarily manipulated via external intervention. This precisely refers to the idea that human behavior could be arbitrarily conditioned, as supported by experiments conducted in animals and humans. However, this concept of learning theory is biased in terms of seeking to control the environment only, while inadequately allowing an explanation of social learning. Bandura's learning theory is based on behavioristic learning theories, does expand those with numerous aspects and does attribute a pivotal role to innerpsychic factors, as well as the interaction between individual and environment. According to Bandura, learning is a process that allows for active and cognitive processing of experiences, combined with the ability to learn from the experiences of others (symbolic and substitutional learning). Human learning comprises processes of motivation, sensation, and thought. Symbolic, substitutional and self-regulatory processes are of central importance here. Human beings learn by observing the behavior of other humans, but also the consequences ensuing their behavior: „Die Fähigkeit, durch Beobachtung zu lernen, ermöglicht den Menschen ausgedehnte, integrierte Verhaltensmuster zu erwerben, ohne sie langwierig und mühsam durch Versuch und Irrtum aufbauen zu müssen." (The ability to learn from observation imparts the human being the ability to acquire expansive, integrated behavior patterns, foregoing the need to tediously and arduously build them through trial and error. Bandura, A.: Sozial-kognitive Lerntheorie. Stuttgart: Klett-Cotta. 1979, p. 22). Not only does observational learning enable the human being to immediately internalize behavioral patterns, but according to Bandura this skill is vital for survival. The conception that appropriate behavior patterns are the result of their consequences and are discovered through success or failure can have fatal ramifications, for example when learning how to drive a car. In this situation, possible mistakes can even be deadly. The essential realization of the social cognitive learning theory is that learning does not solely occur through direct experience of contingencies, but also through watching other people. Bandura observed that human behavior is largely relayed through social role models. Social role models include not only real models (for example teachers or parents), but also symbolic models (for example the media), through which social learning can occur. Based on this belief, Bandura developed the theory of modeled learning, which will be addressed in more detail later.

At first, Bandura assumes that the human behavioral repertoire is not inborn, but has to be learned through own or observed experiences. Moreover, behavioral patterns are influenced in their potential by genetic conditions. Nonetheless, Bandura postulates it is impossible to explain behavior patterns alone with theories of heredity or the environment. Bandura is in fact convinced „(...) dass die Einflüsse aus Erfahrung und Physiologie auf vielfältige Weise interagieren und so das Verhalten bestimmen. Sie lassen sich deshalb kaum voneinander scheiden." (... that the effects of experience and physiology interact in various ways and so determine behavior. Hence, they can be barely distinguished from each other. Bandura, A.: Sozial-kognitive Lerntheorie. Stuttgart: Klett-Cotta. 1979, p. 25). Furthermore, Bandura refrains from separating inherent and learned behavior and rather seeks the explanation of a complex behavioral pattern in the analysis of its combined determinants. Learning by reinforcement is according to Bandura a vital aspect in learning and retaining certain behaviors, while others are discarded. Human behavior is guided by the consequences it elicits. These can be positive (success, praise, acknowledgement) or negative (failure, disdain, punishment, trouble) and affect subsequent behavior: „Durch diesen Prozess differenzierter Bekräftigung werden schließlich erfolgreiche Verhaltensweisen ausgewählt und unbrauchbare aufgegeben." (Through this process of differentiated reinforcement, successful behavioral patterns are eventually adopted and useless ones are abandoned. Bandura, A.: Sozial-kognitive Lerntheorie. Stuttgart: Klett-Cotta. 1979, p. 26).

Bandura attributes three central functions to reactional consequences: the informative, the motivational and the affirmative function.

The informative function: due to their behavior, respectively their reactions, human beings gain information about the effects their reactions leave behind und consequently realize which course of action is appropriate for a given situation and select satisfactory conduct over non-satisfactory: „Die Kognitionen werden also selektiv durch differenzierte Konsequenzen gestärkt oder widerlegt, die in einem gewissen zeitlichen Abstand auf die Reaktionen folgen." (Thus, cognitions are selectively strengthened or refuted due to differentiated consequences ensuing the reactions within a certain interval of time. Bandura, 1979. p. 26). This processing of information happens via cognitively regulated processes and can lead to a modification of behavior, provided the acting person is cognizant which type of behavior will also be reaffirmed in the future. Motivational functions serve to look out for behavioral consequences in the future. When a person experiences consequences due to own behavior, a set of expectations opposite future behavioral consequences in similar situations is developed, as well as the ability to evaluate those as promising or ineffective and steer clear of unpleasant situations. This insight can create behavioral motivation, simultaneously existing with proactive thinking and leading to the adjustment of present behavior to future situations. Affirmative functions allow for the probability to rise, that the affirmed behavior would occur more frequently and is apt to regulate already learned behavior patterns. However, they do not sufficiently explain how behavioral patterns are learned.

2.2. Learning from role models

The central idea of the social cognitive learning theory is the theory of learning from role models (modeling), putting forward the assumption that social learning primarily occurs through imitation of others. Synonyms like modeled learning, observational learning, imitative learning, copy learning, role model learning, or substitutional learning are frequently used for this learning theory. The definition of a role model is rather broad. With reference to the social cognitive learning theory, a model embodies „jegliche Repräsentation eines Verhaltensmusters" (any representation of a behavior pattern; Lefrancois, G.: Psychologie des Lernens. Berlin, u.a.: Springer. 1994, p. 200). This signifies that a model can be any entity presenting behavioral patterns that can be imitated and independently performed by the observer. Human beings can be models amongst themselves, whereby various possible combinations (also with respect to role relations) are applicable: „Menschen dienen als Modelle für andere Menschen, Eltern dienen als Modelle für ihre Kinder, Kinder dienen als Modelle für andere Kinder und manchmal für Erwachsene, und Erwachsene imitieren einander fortwährend." (Human beings serve as role models for other human beings, parents serve as role models for their children, children serve as role models for other children and sometimes for adults, and adults imitate each other continuously. Lefrancois, G.: Psychologie des Lernens. Berlin, u.a.: Springer. 1994, p. 200). These kinds of models are usually termed realistic models, whereas symbolic models can be for example the media in television, film, literature, and the like. Moreover, modeling involves on the one hand the representation of the modeling behavior by the role model and on the other the learning from the model by the observer. A complex process of imitation lies between role model and observer. This process can elicit three distinct effects: learning through modeling (modeling effect), repressive and disinhibitory effects, as well as triggering effects (according to Lefrancois, G.: Psychologie des Lernens. Berlin, u.a.: Springer. 1994, p. 200- 202).

When an observer is imitating behavior and as a result thereof is adopting new behavioral and reactional patterns into the own behavioral repertoire, educational scientists and psychologists speak of modeled learning. A condition of modeled learning is that such displayed behavior was not evident or not mastered before the learning process took place.

Another effect of imitation is inhibition or disinhibition of behavior patterns, which is closely related with the consequences of model behavior. If modeling behavior is rewarded (positive consequences), it is more likely that this behavior will be imitated (disinhibition). If modeling behavior is punished (negative consequences), similar behavior by the observer can be suppressed (inhibition).

The third effect that can occur in the course of the imitation process is the triggering effect. It can manifest itself when behavior is not newly acquired and not identically imitated by the observer, but is rather similar to the model behavior and serves as an incentive for the observer to act in the same manner (for example general character traits, like kindness, ambition, helpfulness, etc.).

It should be mentioned here, that the human being does not imitate just any behavior tied to positive consequences by default. If this would apply, Bandura's theory could be attributed to environmental determinism, which Bandura did explicitly reject. What, how and from whom is being copied, is largely associated with cognitive processes, the core aspect of which is self-control.

As pertains to modeled learning, Bandura distinguishes the adoption phase and the execution phase and assumes further cognitive processes for these phases, respectively. The adoption phase can also be referred to as the acquisition or learning phase and the execution phase as imitation or behavior phase. Hence, according to Bandura, there is a learning process taking place before this is established through behavior (see Mietzel, G.: Psychologie in Unterricht und Erziehung. Göttingen, u.a.: Hogrefe. 1993, p. 118). These assumptions can be visualized by means of an experiment that Bandura conducted. In three separate rooms groups of four- to five-year-old children were shown a movie, in which the actor, respectively model (an adult) was displaying aggressive behavior towards a puppet. The three different groups of children were shown different versions of the ending for the movie. In one version the aggressive behavior of the actor led to positive consequences (praise, acknowledgement by other people). In the second version the actor's behavior was punished and in the third version the aggressive behavior had no consequences. Subsequently, the children were led in a room together and observed while playing. The scientists noted, that children who were exposed to aggressive behavior being rewarded, showed distinct imitating behavior, this in contrast to children who saw in the movie that aggressive behavior was punished or had no consequences. However, these differences in behavior between the groups of children disappeared, when they were promised a reward for good imitation behavior. Ultimately all children imitated the previously observed aggressive behavior. The adoption phase characterizes a learning process, in which the observer sees and learns optional behavior by means of a model. Since, however, a person does not imitate indiscriminately, a model has to have a certain relevance for the observer, which will determine the choice of model and behavior to imitate. Bandura hypothesizes that attentional processes, as partial processes, control observational learning. The observer is subjected to a magnitude of influences, among which certain characteristics are selected and considered, while others in turn receive no attention: „Einige dieser Faktoren sind Merkmale der Beobachter, andere sind Eigenarten der modellierten Tätigkeit selbst, und wieder andere hängen mit der Struktur menschlicher Interaktionen zusammen." (Some of these factors are traits of the observers, others are peculiarities of the modeled activity itself, and others again have to do with the structure of human interaction. Bandura, A.: Sozial- kognitive Lerntheorie. Stuttgart: Klett- Cotta. 1979, p. 33). Social interactions play an important role here, as they determine to a large extent, which behavior is noticed and observed by who and how often, and on whom and what a person's attention is focussed. Consequently, it can be assumed that paying attention is dependent upon values of functionality and attractiveness that a model has for the observer.

Attractive models (realistic, as well as symbolic) can be found in various domains, for example within a social group: a clique of peers (peer-group), in which some personalities get more attention than others due to successful behavior (for example group leaders, who enjoy great popularity), or also at school (this subject will be discussed in detail later). Various behavioral patterns can be conveyed through mass media, attracting a great deal of attention from children and adults (for example attractive movie actors, beauty ideals and many more). In general terms, a thesis can be put forward that the attention can focus on any perceivable model, which in various ways is attractive and useful for the observer. Moreover, the focus of attention is a function of the observer's attitude for perception and ability to process information. In order for a model to have a sustainable impact on the observer's behavior „(...) die Reaktionsmuster symbolisch im Gedächtnis repräsentiert sein." (... the reaction patterns have to be symbolically represented in memory. Bandura, A.: Sozial- kognitive Lerntheorie. Stuttgart: Klett-Cotta. 1979, p. 34). As another condition for modeled learning, Bandura suggests retaining processes, according to which the observed activities manifest themselves in the observer's memory, even if this activity is not perceived immediately. Thus, the modeled behavior is supposed to be stored and be retrievable in the observer's perception over a longer period of time. Memory can store events for the longer term, if they are translated into symbols (mental images, symbols of speech) and restructured (cognitive organisation). Moreover, an event can be repeated in the form of mental and linguistic symbols by the observer imagining to perform the modeled behavior himself.

Observational learning can only take place, when the observed actions are actually implemented, i.e. executed by the observer. Bandura speaks of the motor-reproduction process as part of the performance phase. An important distinction to be made is between acquisition and performance phases, since it has to be assumed that a person does not perform everything he learns and that not every observation is transformed into independent action. When a person observes the behavior of other human beings, he has to possess certain motor-abilities in order to copy this behavior. Repeated observation of the modeled behavior pattern is beneficial to improve and adjust a possibly erroneously memorized behavior pattern to the behavior of the model. Bandura assumes a „(...) Diskrepanz zwischen der symbolischen Repräsentation und der tatsächlichen Ausführung (...)" (descrepancy between the symbolic representation and the actual performance, Bandura, A.: Sozial-kognitive Lerntheorie. Stuttgart: Klett- Cotta. 1979, p. 37). Hereby cues or reactions by other observers (i.e. suggestions for improvement) can result in approaching the behavior one aims to achieve. According to Bandura, the motor-ability to reproduce behavior patttterns involves four requirements: the observer has to possess 1. certain physical abilities and 2. partial reactions that are necessary for performing this activity. In order to correct possibly flawed imitations, the performer has to observe himself performing. Since this is only partially possible, he does rely on feedback from the outside.

In order for humans wanting to perform a behavior in the first place and to add it to their existing behavioral repertoire, motivation is needed, i.e. the behavior has to be attractive and valuable, just like the associated behavioral consequences. The motivational process follows predictable reinforcements. If the observer assumes that the modeled behavior entails positive consequences, he will more likely imitate this behavior, as compared to behavior for which he would have to expect punishment, for example. Substitutional reinforcement means that the observer can see, how the model receives positive consequences following the behavior, which in turn is an experience serving him as an incentive to adopt this behavior. Hence, the observer does not necessarily have to experience reinforcement, but can observe it with another person. Reinforcements, respectively affirmations can be external or originate with the observer himself. External affirmation means that the observer is offered attractive stimuli from the outside for producing the modeled behavior. When a mother promises ice cream to her child, if the child produces the previously observed activity of learning how to ride a bike on her own (provided, the ice cream is an attractive stimulus for the child, who is supposed to learn riding a bike), Bandura speaks of external reinforcement. However, the observer can also self-affirm, further his behavior, align with his behavioral standards, and create behavior consequences on his own (self-affirmation). Since according to Bandura, the human being is not defined by his environment, he implies that humans navigate and regulate their behavior on their own. In the context of the social cognitive learning theory, self-control of behavior implies, „wenn ein Individuum selbst Maßnahmen ergreift, die bei ihm eine Verhaltensänderung im Gefolge haben." (when an individual takes measures on his own, that result in a change of his behavior. Mietzel, G.: Psychologie in Unterricht und Erziehung. Göttingen u.a.: Hogrefe. 1993, p. 122). Self-control is associated with decision-making processes. Thus, an individual has to decide, how to currently comport himself in view of which future consequences follow his current behavior. Possibly the current behavior can be unpleasant, however, can have a positive effect on future consequences. For example: A student skips leisure activities with friends in the afternoon, but instead prepares for an important presentation at school. The student does not like the decision not to play with his friends. But he knows that if he does not focus on the presentation, there will be negative outcomes at school. However, he would like to get a good grade for his performance.

Bandura assumes that self-control involves processes of self-observation, self-assessment, and of self-defined behavior consequences. Self-observation serves the goal of making aware of the own behavior. This can be done, for example, by making a protocol. The own behavior is evaluated on the basis of what a person expects of himself and what is desirable for him. He sets performance standards to guide his behavior. The expectations that people formulate for themselves are the product of observing other people and of own experiences. Hereby it is relevant, however, which interests someone pursues and what significance separate disciplines have, in order to set high or low expectations for oneself.

Bandura researched how the development of behavior and performance standards takes place. He concluded that in particular the influence of adults is of prime importance for the development of children's performance standards. Children who did observe an adult setting high expectations for himself when tackling a challenge, in real situations likewise set high expectations for themselves. In contrast, children would set low expectations for themselves and were more likely satisfied with their performances, when their role model did the same. In this context, modeled learning took place. Individuals who set high expectations for their performances are more likely inclined to be dissatisfied, while individuals who set low expectations more readily accept their accomplishments. Satisfaction or dissatisfaction with the own performance largely determines, if an individual will reward or punish himself for his behavior. Hence, there is a connection with expectations. When the expectations regarding the own performance are perceived as being met in a satisfactory manner, a person can reward himself (for example go on a break, tend to other attractive activities). When the expectations are not met, a person is dissatisfied and does not affirm his accomplishments. According to Bandura, the contingent self-affirmation is pivotal for reaching additional goals.

2.3. Theory of behavior modification

The theory of behavior modification in general gravitates around the question, how modeled learning can be systematically applied to aberrant behavior. This approach is predominantly used in behavior therapy: „In der deutschen Literatur versteht man unter Verhaltensmodifikation ebenfalls die kontrollierte lernpsychologische Beeinflussung von Problemverhalten, verwendet den Begriff aber vorzugsweise für therapeutische Behandlungen in der sozialen Umwelt (Familie, Schule, Heime, Kindergarten) unter der Einbeziehung der Bezugspersonen des Klienten." (In the German literature, behavior modification is likewise understood as the controlled learning psychology-based intervention for problematic behavior, although the term is primarily used for therapeutic treatment options in the social environment (family, school, daycare centers, kindergarten) with the inclusion of the caregiver for the client.) (Bauer: Verhaltensmodifikation durch Modellernen. Stuttgart, u.a.: Kohlhammer. 1979, p. 18).

Bandura assumes that the individual constantly interacts with his environment. Thereby the factors like environment, behavior and cognitive, innerpsychic processes play an important role, as they affect each other (reciprocal determinants) and interact with each other. On one hand, the individual is under the influence of the environment, and on the other hand the individual's behavior has an effect on his environment. As was demonstrated with the aforementioned experiment by Bandura (see chapter Learning from a role model; aggression forming experiment), aggressive behavior can be acquired through learning from a role model. Bandura also investigated treatment methods for animal phobias and employed the model-directed learning approach for therapeutic purposes (whereby behavior modification of a variety of aberrant behavior can be applied). In order to therapeutically and systematically change abnormal behavior, Bandura described following methods (compare Lefrancois, G.: Psychologie des Lernens. Berlin, u.a.: Springer. 1994, p. 202- 204):

Positive reinforcement (based on operant conditioning): The patient is rewarded for every desired behavior (reinforced). The desired behavior is supposed to be evoked by the therapist and is subsequently reinforced by the therapist.

Counterconditioning: Is primarily used in therapies targeting fears or phobias and employs the basic technique of systematic desensitizing, i.e. slowly being introduced to a desired behavior. At first, the patient explains which situations do cause him fear. Subsequently he learns a technique that is incompatible with the fearful reaction (for example relaxation techniques). The patient is supposed to relax and is confronted with stimuli, which he claimed would cause him fear (from weakest to strongest stimulus). If the person does still sense fear, the stimulus is removed and the patient is asked to relax again. The procedure is repeated until the confrontation with the stimulus does not cause any reaction of fear.

Deletion: Undesired behavior can be eliminated, when positively reinforcing factors leading to this behavior, are turned off. If a child would like to draw more attention, for example by running during class time, this behavior can be eradicated by the teacher not giving any attention to this behavior.

Learning through observation: Based on modeling effects that occur with learning through observation. A child can acquire desired behavior through modeled learning, when a role model is demonstrating the desired behavior to him (informative effect). Through observation of others and their behavior consequences, the child can be discouraged (inhibitory effect) or motivated to perform the same behavior. Alternatively, the child is shown a model having great relevance for him (triggering effect).

Discriminatory learning: Patients should learn to distinguish between stimuli and situations, where their behavior is appropriate or inappropriate.

Behavior modification is suitable for therapeutic purposes, like the overcoming of fears (ex. exam anxiety), compulsive behavior, severe behavioral deficits, pathological social behavior, insecurities (ex. self-confidence training), or aggressive behavior.

3. Social-psychological aspects in school and instruction

Social psychology is a branch of psychology and is generally investigating social processes, structures, and relationships between individuals and their environment, in particular the behavior, emotions, and cognition of human beings in social situations. This chapter will focus on social psychologiey in the school setting, i.e. describe social-psychological processes that should be encountered and analyzed within the institution of the school and in the classroom.

Children and youth go to school, where they meet other children, youth, and teachers in an institutional framework. School has the substantial task of education, but also the function of socialisation. In class, children and youth are joined in a school class system that they usually cannot shape and are taught under the instruction of a teacher, with the goal to learn. Often, children, youth, and teachers spend an extended period of time together. The following chapters aim to explain in detail with respect to the perspective of students and the teacher, what sort of social structures, processes, and interactions can emerge in school and instruction.

3.1. Social relationships in the classroom

Klaus Ulich defines the classroom as follows: „Die Schulklasse ist nach wie vor ein außerordentlich wichtiger sozialer Erfahrungsraum, in dem Kinder und Jugendliche Beziehungen zu Gleichaltrigen eingehen können und z.T. auch müssen, indem sie sich mit anderen vergleichen, anfreunden oder mit ihnen konkurrieren können." (The classroom remains an extremely important social sphere for experiences, in which children and youth can form relationships with peers and in part are pressured, while they compare themselves with others, to become friends, or can compete with them. Ulich, K.: Einführung in die Sozialpsychologie der Schule. Weinheim, Basel: Beltz Verlag. 2001, p. 50). Hence, the classroom is a system of peers, institutionalized and created by society, where the joining does not happen voluntarily, but is implemented according to measures of societal organization. This implies that children and youth have to get along in the classroom, whether they want to or not. With regard to the unvoluntary nature of class formation, different relationships among the students can be noticed. So, for example, the formation of cliques is possible, i.e. voluntary formation of smaller groups within the class, whose members have befriended each other. Then again, aggression, bullying, or mobbing towards other students, and also classmates surface quite often. Interactions between students can occur in varying degrees, dependent on the roles they play in the classroom. At school or within a classroom there are frequently students, who are very popular and respected and who many students seek out to befriend. Normally, these are students who play group leader roles. Their behavior patterns are more likely accepted and respected. Students who are not sufficiently integrated in such groups, are often outsiders who receive little attention and are for various reasons ostracized (whereby it has to be assumed that not every classroom fits this generalized structure).

Developmental psychologists found „(…) dass Kinder und Jugendliche durch ihre Kontakte mit Gleichaltrigen Erfahrungen sammeln, die für ihre kognitive und soziale Entwicklung von größter Bedeutung sind." (that through their contacts with peers, children and youth make experiences that are of greatest significance for their cognitive and social development. Mietzel, G.: Psychologie in Unterricht und Erziehung. Göttingen u.a.: Hogrefe. 1993, p. 292). The theses of social cognitive learning find application here. Bandura emphasized that behavioral patterns largely are based on own or observed experiences of others. Moreover, it is important to consider, how often an observer has the opportunity to notice a model (importance of social interactions) and which model is deemed worthy of imitation (attractive and useful model). For the most part, classes are formed over several years as stable group ties. Additionally, students in a class spend several hours with each other on a daily basis. They are not only together during instruction, but also for extracurricular activities, like day trips or class trips. Consequently, students have many opportunities to observe each other, notice and evaluate behavior. Students can serve as models among their peers, a situation which can arise in various circumstances, for which there are numerous examples.

One example: Student A is friends with student B. Student A observes over a longer period of time, that student B works hard at school and as a result has good grades. For student A good grades are important and therefore he resolves to make an effort in class as well (triggering effect).

3.2. Teacher-student-interaction

The teacher-student-interaction is a critical factor for the quality of instruction, the development of social cognitions and the satisfaction with school and instruction, this on the part of the teacher as well as the students. A number of scientific studies did corroborate this aspect. This chapter will present a few results from research work to the subject of teacher-student-interaction.

At school and in particular in the classroom, teacher and students find themselves in a reciprocal relationship with each other. The behavior of the teacher affects the behavior of the students and vice versa. As for these relationships, they are not voluntarily chosen either. Teachers are assigned to classrooms and the same way students cannot choose their teachers, teachers cannot pick their students. Students and teachers are herewith forced to establish a relationship with each other over a prolonged period of time. Due to school norms, the relationship between teachers and students is relatively uneven. The teacher predominantly takes on a leadership role. Teachers mainly determine the course and contents of instruction, give directives, dispense sanctions or praise, assign or withdraw the students' right to speak, control and evaluate the students' performance and behavior. The teacher-student-interaction is also characterized by the students' dependency on the teacher.

Students attend school primarily for the reason of learning. They learn (predominantly) from the teacher, who conveys knowledge content to them. This does reflect the disparity of the teacher-student-relationship, since the teacher possesses more knowledge than the students and students have to still gain this knowledge. If they do not sufficiently succeed in doing this, bad evaluations and grades are the means to select and (possibly) sanction them. Hence, the teacher is in a position of power opposite the students.

It is not only a general disparity that is evident within the teacher-student-interaction. Interactions between teachers and students are also characterized by different relationships with certain students and certain teachers, respectively. More precisely, there are teachers who are very popular with students and others who are less, just as there are students who are more popular with teachers than others. Modeled after Petillon's studies, Ulich described the possible dependencies of these differentiated relationships. Ulich talks about teachers typecasting students and distinguishes the following types of students (compare Ulich, K.: Einführung in die Sozialpsychologie der Schule. Weinheim, Basel: Beltz. 2001, p. 84- 86):

The ideal student is disciplined, participates in class, displays interest, is frequently praised and receives preferential treatment, and the teacher highlights his behavior as exemplary.

Self-dependent students act rather autonomous and more frequently oppose the teacher, but their academic performance is good. „Lehrer versuchen gegenüber den Selbstständigen häufig, mehr Konformität zu erreichen, indem sie angepasstes Verhalten belohnen, autonomes hingegen eher ignorieren" (Often teachers try to achieve more conformity from the self-dependent student, rewarding conformist but more likely ignoring autonomous behavior. Ulich, 2001, p. 85).

Problem students have a bad performance record, but nevertheless act reasonably in class. Teachers try to encourage these students especially.

Rejected students behave particularly aberrant in class, often receive sanctions from the teacher, and have a bad academic record at school.

Ignored students get little attention from the teacher and have a less intense relationship with the teacher.

Categorizing students primarily depends on expectations, perceptions, and comparison processes by the teacher and in real life is certainly more differentiated than the above-described general typecasting of students. Teachers' expectations in turn have an effect on students' behavior: „Für die Schüler/innen wirken sich insbesondere negative und starre Lehrererwartungen aus, weil ein Verhalten, das solchen Annahmen nicht entspricht, vom Lehrer kaum mehr wahrgenommen wird. Umgekehrt können positive Lehrererwartungen zu einer für beide Seiten angenehmen Interaktion und zum Wohlfühlen der Schüler/innen beitragen." (In particular negative and inflexible expectations by the teacher have an impact on students, because behavior that does not conform with such expectations, is hardly noticed by the teacher. Conversely, positive teacher's expectations can contribute to a pleasant interaction for both sides and to the students' wellbeing. Ulich, 2001, S. 93).

Petillon did find out that there is an impressive correlation between popularity and performance of a student. Students who enjoy popularity with the teacher, often have better grades and less frequently repeat a grade level. This insight is of great significance for Bandura's social cognitive learning theory. School grades can have a reinforcement function. Moreover, the teacher has the power to praise or reprimand students, which in turn affects students' behavior. What is far more crucial at this point is the connection existing between teacher-student-interaction and modeled learning (teacher as model, teacher as role model). In order to determine if, when, and how a teacher can become a model for students, the challenge is to investigate, what kind of experiences students have with teachers, what kind of expectations students have for teachers, and how they evaluate teachers. These questions are closely related with the behavior pattern of a teacher towards the students: „Die unbeliebten spüren, dass andere Schüler/innen mehr gemocht werden. Sie erfahren mehr Ärger, Strenge und Wut der Lehrer/innen, werden von ihnen öfters vor der Klasse blamiert und haben stärker Angst vor ihnen. Jeweils umgekehrt verhält es sich bei den beliebten Schüler/innen, die eindeutig positivere Erfahrungen mit Lehrer/innen machen." (The unpopular students can feel that other students receive preferential treatment. They experience trouble, strictness and outrage by teachers, are more frequently made feel embarrassed in front of the class and have a stronger sense of fear towards the teacher. The opposite is the case for popular students, who clearly have more positive experiences with teachers. Ulich, 2001, p. 98).

Just like teachers, so do students have expectations for the teacher and compare these with teacher behavior. A teacher's characteristics, like professional competence, helpfulness, openness, sincerity, clear work and performance requirements, understanding, equality, etc. are expected by the student and mostly seen as positives. Strictness, authority, injustice, obedience on the other hand, are seen as negatives.

3.3. Social learning in school and instruction

School as an institution does not only have the task of imparting knowledge content in order to qualify children and youth for societal demands. To accomplish the latter goal, school has to convey values and norms as well, meaning that school has an important education and socialization function. Social learning and the acquisition of social competency are an essential aspect of the educational objective. Social learning describes a learning process in social contact with others, like exemplary role models (model-directed learning) and the learning of important behavior patterns (social competency). Social learning supports adequate behavior in all situations of human interaction. Consequently, school and instruction needs to be shaped in a way that allows social learning in respective situations to happen. Social learning at school can take place in various social formats (ex. frontal instruction, work with a partner, group instruction) and requires a didactic concept. During frontal instruction, the students' attention is usually directed towards the teacher. Therefore, instructional content is predominantly conveyed by the teacher, whose statements and behavior are perceived and observed. The implication with regard to social learning is that the teacher can be a model for the students, in particular with sports and foreign language instruction. Working with a partner or in groups can encourage social learning by independently completing a task, developing strategies and plans, or working creatively. Students can learn from each other (students as models for other students), when there are gaps in understanding and they help each other. Montessori-schools in particular promote this working method. Hereby the teacher retreats to the background (sets impulses) and students learn from each other in mixed-age classrooms.

Another concept for social learning includes interaction games, designed to help the students learn appropriate behavior patterns. „IAS sind Verfahren, Übungen, Techniken, Spiele zur Strukturierung einer zeitlich festgelegten Lernsequenz nach speziellen Regeln, um bestimmte (meist soziale oder emotionale) Ziele zu erreichen." (Interaction games are strategies, exercises, techniques, games with the goal to structure a learning sequence according to a set schedule and following specific rules to achieve certain (mostly social or emotional) goals. Heimlich, R.: Soziales und emotionales Lernen in der Schule. Weinheim, Basel: Beltz. 1988, p. 16). Interaction games in the classroom have following functions: have a motivating and inviting effect, promote the autonomous control of behavior and decision-making ability, offer new experiences, tie into own experiences and enable first-hand experiences through self-motivation, have a symbolic character (i.e. behavior consequences are not real) and have integrative functions (for example include social outsiders in the classroom).

3.4. Teacher as model

Previous statements have already suggested that the teacher in the classroom can have a role model function for students. With regard to the social cognitive learning theory, the teacher can be considered a model, while the term of role model is rather found in colloquial language.

Considering the central points in the previous chapters, the following reasons can be listed, as to why a teacher can become a model for a student: Teachers have a great potential to influence students. They have expert knowledge that they try in part to convey to students and which students have to master in order to conform to societal requirements (ex. behavior that is accepted by society, obtain professional qualification). Moreover, teachers have the power of sanction, which can manifest itself in giving bad grades or reprimands, when students do not meet the set performance or behavior standards. Vice versa, the teacher can reinforce desired behavior by giving good grades or praise. In particular with frontal instruction, the teacher draws a great deal of the students' attention on himself and is exposed for observation (attention processes). In addition, teachers spend several hours every day with students. Thus, students can observe teacher behavior at many occasions and in various situations, and can practice to behave in a similar way (retaining processes). Knowledge contents are adjusted to the students' stage of development, so that students have the capabilities to reproduce the observed behavior, for example to copy an exercise the teacher demonstrates during physical education class (reproduction of motor skills). Teachers can motivate students by reinforcing desired student behavior externally, for example with good grades or praise. Substitutional reinforcement can also occur in the classroom, when students observe that the teacher positively reinforces the behavior of a certain student and they in turn get motivated to display this behavior themselves (motivational processes). Teachers can be models to their students concerning their social behavior and their performance. The relationship between model (teacher) and observer (student) is of vital importance for the imitation behavior:

„Geht es nämlich um Verhaltensweisen, die einen Bedürfnisverzicht verlangen, etwa Selbstkritik und Selbstkontrolle (…), altruistisches Handeln (…), oder aggressives Handeln (…), so mindert warme Zuwendung (…), die Nachahmung (…). Offenbar sinken durch die Zuwendung des Vorbilds Sanktionsbefürchtungen der Kinder. Geht es hingegen um Nachahmung neutraler Verhaltensweisen (…) so wirkt Wärme nachahmungsfördernd."

(When it is about behavior patterns that demand to do without, like self-criticism and self-control (...), altruistic behavior (...), or aggressive behavior (...), a warm interaction (...) can diminish the imitation (...). Apparently, the interaction with the role model lowers the children's fear of sanctions. However, is it about the imitation of neutral behavior patterns (...), warmth has the effect of promoting imitation. (Halisch, F.: Beobachtungslernen und die Wirkung von Vorbildern. In: Spada, H. (Hrsg.): Lehrbuch Allgemeine Psychologie. Bern u.a.: Huber. 1990, p. 395 f.).

Thus it is necessary to examine the student-teacher-interaction in a more refined manner, if the intent is to draw a conclusion regarding a relationship with and impact on imitation behavior. In addition, this requires a more refined teacher behavior.

4. Summary: Pedagogical implications of the social cognitive learning theory for school and instruction

The social cognitive learning theory according to Bandura and associated social-psychological aspects offer the deduction of some consequences for school and instruction. Discussions in public education policy circles focus on the role model function of the teacher in instruction and school environments. For instance, most schools enforce a smoking ban for students that likewise applies to teachers, since they do not only have a role model function, but a role model obligation. Another subject of debate among education policy makers is the question, if it is socially acceptable for female teachers to wear a headscarf during class or if this would set an undesirable precedent for students. These debates in education politics presuppose imitation behavior and hence point to the timeliness of the social cognitive learning theory and its significance for school and instruction. In the context of school and instruction, the social cognitive learning theory signifies the following:

Imitation behavior can take place in school and in the classroom using different models, which can be students for each other, but also teachers as models for their students. In particular the teacher should be aware of his model function and shape his own behavior according to what he expects from students. If for example the teacher is expecting his students to be punctual, he himself should be in the classroom on time. Does the teacher expect well-prepared students, he has to display professional competence and teach a well-planned curriculum. Only what can be immediately observed and noticed, can become a model. Hence, the teacher should express cognitive and social contents in a clear, concise, and comprehensible manner. According to Bandura, not every teacher automatically becomes a model, but the observers (students) first have to direct their perception towards the teacher. This is more likely to happen, when the teacher is attractive and valuable for the student and when there is a pleasant teacher-student-relationship. The students' evaluation of the teacher determines if students internalize, memorize, and reproduce contents they are taught.

The teacher as a professional can employ modeled learning in the classroom, using a targeted approach. Models that resemble the observer and are appreciated are more likely to be imitated. Thus, instruction could include student models (ex. in physical education or generally when working in groups).

The goal for instruction should include enabling and motivating as many students as possible to actively participate in the classroom. Activating students in the course of instruction stimulates their ability to pay attention. Without any sufficient motivation, the students will rarely deem instruction as relevant and will possibly not perceive contents correctly, or they will forget quickly.

Literature

- Bandura, A.: Sozial- kognitive Lerntheorie. (Social cognitive learning theory) Stuttgart: Klett- Cotta. 1979

- Bauer, M.: Verhaltensmodifikation durch Modellernen. (Behavior modification through modeled learning) Stuttgart u.a.: Kohlhammer. 1979

- Halisch, F.: Beobachtungslernen und die Wirkung von Vorbildern. (Learning through observation and the effect of role models) In: Spada, H. (Hrsg.): Lehrbuch Allgemeine Psychologie. (Textbook general psychology) Bern u.a.: Huber. 1990

- Heimlich, R.: Soziales und emotionales Lernen in der Schule. (Social and emotional learning at school) Weinheim, Basel: Beltz. 1988

- Lefrancois, G.: Psychologie des Lernens. (Psychology of learning) Berlin u.a. : Springer. 1994

- Mietzel, G.: Psychologie in Unterricht und Erziehung. Einführung in die Pädagogische Psychologie für Pädagogen und Psychologen. (Psychology in instruction and education. Introduction into pedagogical psychology for educators and psychologists) Göttingen u.a.: Hogrefe. 1993

- Ulich, K.: Einführung in die Sozialpsychologie der Schule. (Introduction into social psychology at school) Weinheim, Basel: Beltz. 2001